Silly
FACTS
FOR
Silly
KIDS

You can't **lick** your **elbow**, try it!

The sentence, '**The quick brown fox jumps over the lazy dog**,' contains all the letters of the alphabet!

King Edward II of England attempted to **ban soccer** from being played!

Cows can walk **up** steep stairs but not **down** steep stairs!

Magicians are **forbidden** from telling non-magicians how their magic tricks work!

Racecar spelt backwards spells **racecar**!

If you are **stuck** in a maze, you can find your way out by touching the right hand wall and following it until you exit!

If an earthquake happens on the moon, it is called a **moonquake!**

You can't **sneeze** with your **eyes open!**

You cannot say **"p"** without separating your lips! **Try it!**

No two tigers have the same stripe pattern. Just like fingerprints they are **unique!**

A **hummingbird's** heart rate can reach over **1,200 beats per minute!**

Bananas grow **pointing upwards!**

Over the past few centuries the average human height has **increased!**

Zebras sleep **standing up!**

No English words rhyme with '**orange**' or '**purple**'!

The T-Rex dinosaur went **extinct** 65 million years ago!

Crocodiles **cannot** stick their tongues out at you!

As you grow older your ears **never** stop growing!

Snails can sleep for up to **3 years!**

The pistol shrimp can make a noise with its claw **loud** enough to break glass!

Lizards communicate by doing **push-ups!**

The only lizard that has a voice is the **gecko!**

Scorpions **glow** under ultraviolet light!

Butterflies **taste** things by standing on them!

Moose have **terribly** poor vision!

A **traffic jam** once lasted over 10 days and stretched over 60 miles!

Ants are very strong for their size. Some ants can **lift** more than **100 times** their own weight!

A flea can jump **100 times** its own height!

Hippopotomonstrosesquipedaliophobia, is a fear of **long** words!

Arachibutyrophobia is a fear of **peanut butter** sticking to the roof of your mouth!

A skunk can **accurately** spray its stinky fluid up to 10 feet away!

Sea otters hold hands when sleeping so they don't **drift away** from each other!

Australia has the largest number of **venomous snakes** in the world!

During Medieval times, **animals** could be put on trial for **crimes** in a court of law!

A sneeze can travel up to **100 miles** per hour!

Honey never goes **bad!**

Sailors once thought that the earth was **flat** and that they could **sail off** the **edge!**

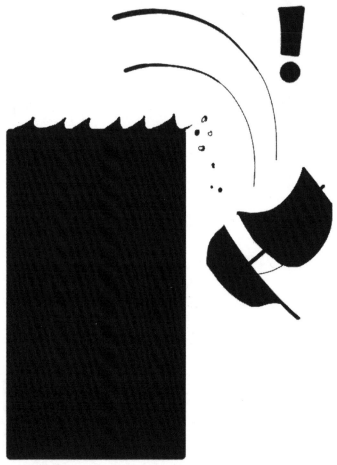

The **theory** that the **Earth is flat** is still believed by some people *around* the **world!**

In a lifetime, an average person will **walk** around the earth 3 times!

Boys are more likely to be struck by **lightning** than **girls!**

Pirates believed that **earrings** could **improve** their eyesight and also prevent sea sickness!

Pirates wore eye patches on one eye so they could easily see in the **darkness** when going under deck where it is **dark!**

Elephants can't jump!

Most of the **dust** in your house is made from dead skin particles! **Yuck!**

Pigs cannot **look up** at the sky!

The octopus has **3 hearts!**

Bamboo can grow nearly **3 feet** a day!

Snakes cannot blink because they have **no eyelids!**

Dolphins **sleep** with one eye open. **Weird!**

You **cannot** hum and hold your nose closed at the same time! **Try it!**

Only the **female mosquito** will bite you!

Hot air is lighter than **cold** air!

The Earth is struck by **lightning** over 100 times every second!

Alligators have very little strength to **open** their mouths but an awesome amount of strength to **shut** them!

Hippos can open their mouths **180 degrees!**

A woodpecker can peck **20 times** per second!

A nautical mile, used for measuring distances on the ocean, is **longer** than a land mile!

Gorillas **cannot** swim!

Gorillas **can** catch human colds!

Ancient Chinese warriors would show off to their enemies by **juggling!**

Computers were once the **size** of a room!

The **Mona Lisa,** a famous painting, has no eyebrows!

Flying fish can jump from the water and glide through the air to escape predators!

A lion's roar can be so **loud** that it can be heard 5 miles away!

There are **more** fake flamingos on Earth than real ones!

There are **119 grooves** on the edge of a US quarter!

Penguins can **jump 6 feet** out of the water!

The **mayfly** only lives for 24 hours!

The seahorse is the **slowest** fish!

The phrase **'blind as a bat'** isn't fair. Some bats can see better than you!

Some **turtles** live to be over 150 years old!

Sound travels **faster** through water than through the air!

The longest dinosaur, **Titanosaur**, was 130 feet in length!

A man once swam down the longest river in the world, the **Amazon River**. It took 66 days!

The United Kingdom's King George IV was so fat that he was given the nickname '**The Prince of Whales**'.

It would take **9 years** to walk to the Moon!

Each year, the Moon moves about 1.5 inches **away** from the Earth!

Outer space is completely **silent** to humans!

There are an **unknown** amount of stars in the universe!

The Sun is large enough to fit **one million** planet Earths inside it!

Pluto was **once** considered a planet!

You become slightly **taller** in space because there is no gravity pulling you down!

A light year is the **distance** traveled by light in a single year, so **one** light year almost equals **6 trillion miles!**

59 days on Earth equal **one** day on Mercury!

Earth's **address** in the cosmos is:

Planet Earth,
Earth-Moon System,
Solar System,
Milky Way Galaxy,
Local Group,
Virgo Supercluster,
Observable Universe.

Saturn's rings are made up of **ice**, **dust** and **tiny rocks!**

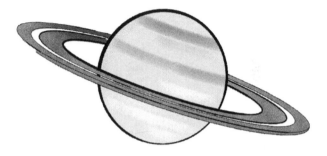

Mars' largest mountain, Olympus Mons, is **3 times** the height of Earth's largest mountain, Mount Everest!

The sun is a **star!**

UFO is short for an **Unidentified Flying Object!**

IFO is short for an **Identified Flying Object!**

The **pyramids** in Egypt were tombs. They contained preserved bodies, known as **mummies**!

Cleopatra was the last pharaoh of Ancient Egypt!

In England, during the 1880's, **'pants'** was considered a dirty word!

The **praying mantis** is the only insect that can turn its head!

An elephant's large ears help keep its body **cool!**

Dogs **do not** sweat!

The hottest temperature ever recorded in **Antarctica** is 59 °F!

Boy birds are the colorful and pretty ones!

Every ton of **recycled paper** saves about **17** trees!

The tongue is the **fastest** healing part of the body!

The Scottish national animal is a **unicorn!**

The New Zealand **Air Force** logo features the kiwi bird, a **flightless** bird!

Both Ancient Egyptian **men** and **women** wore makeup!

Hurricanes, **typhoons** and **cyclones** are the same type of storm but are named according to **where** they take place!

Australia is the only continent with no active volcanoes!

There are more **kangaroos** in Australia than **people!**

Antarctica is the only continent without reptiles or snakes!

Not all deserts are hot and full of sand. Antarctica has the **world's largest** desert!

Bubble wrap was originally designed as **wall paper!**

The **tomato** is a **fruit!**

The **mimic octopus** can change colors and **copy** the shapes of other sea creatures!

The **'Happy birthday'** song is the world's most sung song!

The woolly mammoth was still **alive** when the pyramids were built!

A shark's sense of **smell** is 1000 times better than yours!

You **cannot** spot the difference between a koala fingerprint and a human fingerprint!

Koalas **sleep** 18 hours a day!

March 14th is **'Save a Spider Day'**!

The plastic tips at the ends of your shoelaces are called **aglets!**

A **jellyfish** is mostly made of water and **does not** have a **brain!**

The most **commonly** used **letter** in the alphabet is **E!**

The opposite sides of a dice add up to **7!**

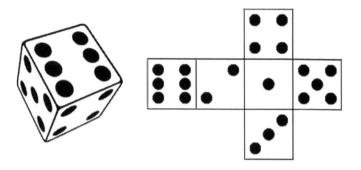

In the past, a **headache** would be cured by **drilling a hole** in your **head.** Ow!

A cricket's ears are found on its **front legs!**

The **ostrich** can run faster than a **horse**!

An ostrich's brain is **smaller** than one of its eyes!

Once a year in the U.K., competitors will chase a roll of **cheese** down a steep hill. The winner keeps the cheese!

The Border Collie is one of the **smartest** dog breeds in the world!

The **sun** is 4.5 billion years old!

The average **golf ball** has **336 dimples** on it. The dimples helps the ball travel **farther!**

The world's fastest man can run 100 meters in **under** 10 seconds!

The longest professional tennis match lasted **over 11 hours!**

Tennis originated during Medieval France when it was played with **bare hands!**

3 Olympic Games have been held in countries that no longer **exist!**

Russia is the **largest country** on the world!

The world's smallest country is the **Vatican.** It is **smaller** than New York City's Central Park!

Chess Boxing is a sport where opponents play **chess** and **box** in the **same match!**

The last letter added to the English alphabet was **'J'!**

Hawaii is home to the **only** royal palace in the USA!

The **largest music concert** in history had a crowd of 3,500,000!

111,111,111 x 111,111,111 =
12,345,678,987,654,321

There are **775 rooms** in Britain's Buckingham Palace!

Camels have **straight** spines, despite their curved humps!

Saint Patrick, the patron saint of **Ireland,** was born in **Scotland!**

Rotten eggs **float** in cold water, while good eggs **sink** in cold water!

The **Empire State Building**, in New York City, has **1,860** steps from street level to the 102nd floor!

Your skin is your body's **largest organ!**

Italy's **Leaning Tower of Pisa** only started leaning after construction due to the **soft ground** under one side of the tower!

The **Great of Wall of China** was built to protect China against **invasions!**

You use **17 muscles** to smile and **43 muscles** to frown!

Some submarines can remain submerged under water for months!

In Svalbard, **Norway**, there is no sunset from mid-April to late August. It is consistently **daylight!**

Some buildings do not have a 13th floor because some believe that the number 13 is **unlucky!**

The dragon is a **mythical creature** that has appeared in many **separate** ancient cultures from around the world! Could dragons be real?

The human body has **over** 600 muscles!

One **quarter** of the bones in an adult body are found in the **feet!**

An elephant can produce a **7 gallon pile** of poop! **Ewww!**

The average person uses the bathroom **6 times** a day!

In a lifetime, the average human produces 25,000 quarts of spit. That's enough spit to fill **two swimming pools!**

A cow can produce **40 glasses of milk** per day!

The **queen of England** does **not** need a **passport** to travel!

Queen Elizabeth II employs someone to wear her **shoes** before she wears them to ensure that they are **comfortable!**

In Japan, false teeth were once made of **wood!**

The **toothbrush** existed *waaaaay* back in Ancient Egypt!

Owls **cannot** move or roll their eyes. They need to move their **entire head** to look in a direction!

Brazil has over **4,000 airports!**

The world's smallest bird is the **bee hummingbird.** It can **sit** on top of a **pencil!**

Hummingbirds can fly **backwards!**

An **emu** cannot walk **backwards!**

Giraffes are the tallest animals in the world!

The **smallest bone** in your body is found in your **ear**!

In a deck of cards, the **King of Hearts** is the only king without a mustache!

Paper money was first used in China!

The Ancient Romans used pee for whitening their **teeth!**

A **Roman emperor** once planned to give his favorite horse the **highest position** in government!

The world's **largest gold nugget** weighed approximately 200 pounds!

Brontophobia is the fear of **thunderstorms!**

Fingernails grow **faster** than toenails!

Eating **snails** in France is considered yummy!

The French also eat **frog legs**!

In some Asian countries people eat fried **grasshoppers**, **cockroaches** and **tarantulas**!

In Iceland you can eat a **rotten shark**!

Many lizards are able to **shed their tails** when in danger!

A woman once traveled down Niagara Falls in a **barrel**…. and survived!

A man once traveled down Niagara Falls on a **jet sk**i…. he did not survive.

Austria, not France, invented the **croissant!**

A commercial **airplane** has a cruising speed
of **550 miles per hour!**

Australia is not only an **island** and a **country**, but it is also a **continent!**

Babies are born **without** kneecaps!

Surfing is an official sport of **Hawaii!**

The dot above an **'i'** is called a **tittle!**

Broccoli is a vegetable but is also a flower!

The voice **inside** your head cannot be heard by anybody else!

In the U.S. state of Kentucky, it is **illegal** to fish with a **bow** and **arrow!**

In the U.S. state of Kansas, it's **against** the law to **catch fish** with your **bare hands!**

In the U.S. state of Tennessee, it is illegal to use a **lasso** to catch a fish!

The **firefly** is **not** a **fly** but a beetle, and it tastes **disgusting!**

The **handshake** started in ancient times for people to show strangers that they were unarmed!

Some clubs have **secret** handshakes!

S.O.S. is an international distress signal used with **Morse code!**

People from **Switzerland** eat the most chocolate per person per year!

The French eat the most **cheese** per person in the world!

Chinese is the **most** spoken language in the world!

Movie trailers were once played **after** the movies, that's why they are called *'trailers'*!

A **chameleon's tongue** is twice the length of its body!

Saudi Arabia has **no** rivers!

Peanuts **are not** nuts. They are legumes, like peas and beans!

There are **no snakes** in **Ireland!**

Ireland is believed to be the **birthplace** of **Halloween!**

The first Jack O' Lanterns were made from **turnips!**

A **rainbow** can only be seen in the morning or late afternoon!

Although rare, there are reported cases of fish falling from the **sky!**

Native Americans invented popcorn! **Pop Pop!**

Fortune cookies were actually invented in the United States of America, not China!

The **bullfrog** never sleeps, it just rests!

People in the town of Coober Pedy **live underground** to escape the extreme heat!

A group of **frogs** is called an **army**!

A group of **rhinos** is called a **crash!**

A group of **kangaroos** is called a **mob**!

A male kangaroo is called a **boomer** and a female kangaroo is called a **flyer**!

Karate is a Japanese word meaning empty hand!

Animals that lay eggs do not have **belly buttons!**

There is a spider in South America called the **Goliath Birdeater**. It is the size of your hand and can eat a bird!

The Eiffel Tower was built as a **temporary** structure in 1889, but it still stands today!

To grow potatoes, you plant **potatoes** in the ground, not **seeds!**

Everything is the universe is either a **jelly bean** or not a **jelly bean!**

The End

Also Available:

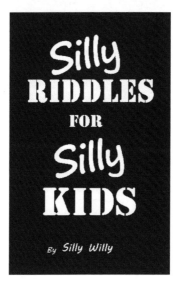

Made in the USA
Middletown, DE
04 March 2018